Autumn at Notforgotten Farm

Needlework Projects to Warm Your Hands and Heart

By Lori Brechlin

Autumn at Notforgotten Farm
Needlework Projects to Warm your Hands and Heart
By Lori Brechlin

Editor: Jenifer Dick
Designer: Sarah Mosher
Photography: Aaron T. Leimkuehler
Illustration: Eric Sears
Technical Editor: Mary Atherton
Photo Editor: Jo Ann Groves

Published by:
Kansas City Star Books
1729 Grand Blvd.
Kansas City, Missouri, USA 64108

All rights reserved
Copyright © 2013 Lori Brechlin and The Kansas City Star Co.

No part of this book may be reproduced, stored in a retrieval system, or transmitted in any form or by any means, electronic, mechanical, photocopying, recording or otherwise, without the prior consent of the publisher.

No finished projects featured in this book can be produced or sold commercially without the permission of the author and publisher.

POD Edition
ISBN: 978-1-61169-102-3

Library of Congress Control Number: 2013944277

Kansas City Star Quilts is an imprint of C&T Publishing, Inc., P.O. Box 1456, Lafayette, CA 94549. ctpub.com

Kansas City Star Quilts

Photos for Autumn at Notforgotten Farm were taken at the Greenwood Antique Mall and Country Tea Room in Greenwood, Mo.

Contents

4 Acknowledgments	**24** Gathering Basket
5 Introduction	**30** Autumn
8 Basic Instructions	**36** September's Blessing
11 Supplies	**40** Calico Shoe Thimble Keep
12 Bittersweet	**44** Old Farmhouse
16 Squash Blossom	**48** About the Author
20 Turkey Trot	

Acknowledgments

I have so many people to thank for their constant support and encouragement of letting me be who I am. Here are only a few.

My husband, Peter — forever by my side — coaxing, guiding and pushing me along. You encouraged me to take this path, and I'll forever be grateful for that. Thank you for choosing me.

My daughter, Hannah — you were the reason I quit my "day job" to spend all of my time with you — and you are the sweet face I see when I close my eyes. Teaching you to work with needle and thread when you were little gave me the confidence to teach others. Thank you for being the best friend/daughter a mom could hope for.

My mom, Elda Smith — remembering the hours watching you crochet, stitch and sew. You helped me discover the pleasures of being quiet and busy with my hands. Thank you for loving me.

My sisters, Sharon and Louisea — even across the miles, we continue to connect and support each other. You have both been a guiding force to me, and I want to be just like you when I grow up. Thank you for answering your phone when I constantly call to chat.

My friends, Felicia and Joan — you are both in my heart and I treasure our friendship. Thank you for always lending a helping hand and for not letting me get too crazy.

Everyone at the Kansas City Star Books for allowing me to share what I love with so many. Thank you for the opportunity.

My fellow stitchers and handworkers — please know that I value each and every one of you who purchase my patterns or finished folk art. It fills my heart to know there are so many who love to work with our hands. It is your continued support that keeps me designing the things we love so much.

— *I am blessed.*

Relax, enjoy the process of gathering your supplies, finding just the right chair to sit in while you work.

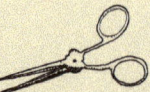

Introduction

I find myself traveling to a simpler place in time — for some reason my heart is firmly planted in this old farmhouse of ours, and in its surrounding fields, woods and pasture.

I often daydream about the women who may have lived here long ago — how they must have loved it as I do today and how they may have used their hands to create simple needlework projects to cozy it up.

The inspiration for this book came from this very place and these very thoughts.

I love Autumn, with its warm days and cold nights, the smell of wood smoke in the crisp air and the sight of changing leaves.

I prefer working with natural materials, such as wool, cotton and linen, and I hope the projects I've included for you here show my love for my favorite season.

The *Bittersweet* ditty bag can be used to hold drieds from your garden or fresh bittersweet as well.

Squash Blossom is the name I chose for the cotton fabric and wool appliqué runner. Every year we grow a small patch of squash and pumpkins and enjoy watching their vines creep along the ground.

Autumn banner hangs on my mantel and welcomes my very favorite season in cotton and wool.

The *Gathering Basket* hooked wool chair pad was inspired by our ever-growing bittersweet bush outside our farmhouse doors. The color of its berries is a staple in my palette.

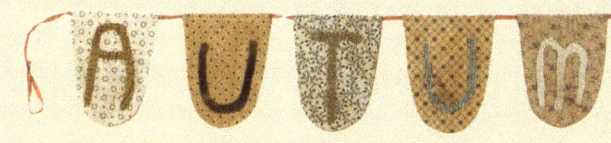

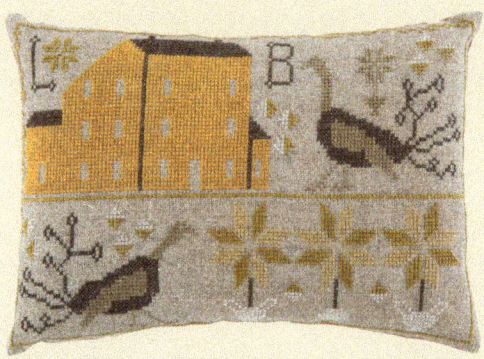

Turkey Trot sawdust pillow, a small sawdust-filled cross stitched pillow, was designed in honor of our wild turkeys that live in our woods. Their long and lanky necks and lack of flying skills keep us entertained every Fall.

The **Old Farmhouse** sampler cross stitch sawdust pillow design was inspired by our humble little farmhouse. You can add your own family initials to personalize it.

I love the pumpkins growing from the basket in the **September's Blessing** cross stitch sampler. And I love the little girl and tiny dog and just the overall simplicity of this design. I chose to finish it by mounting it onto a pumpkin-colored striped wool and framing it in a hand painted frame.

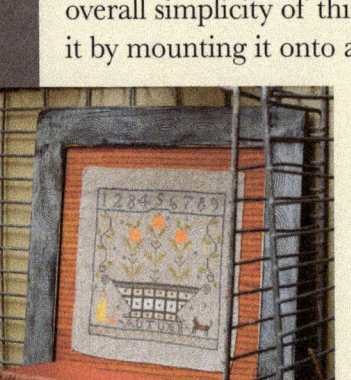

The **Calico Shoe Thimble Keep** necklace is just a little something to help hold your thimble and stray pins while working — a small project that is big on charm!

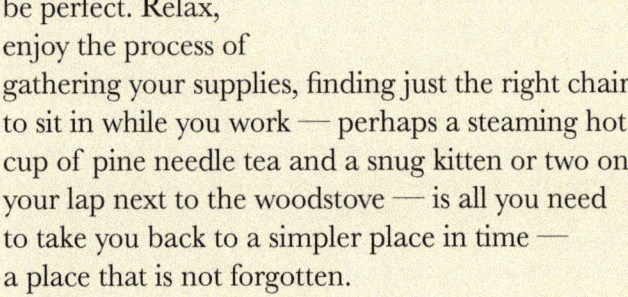

Always remember that handwork is something to be enjoyed — not rushed, and it shouldn't have to be perfect. Relax, enjoy the process of gathering your supplies, finding just the right chair to sit in while you work — perhaps a steaming hot cup of pine needle tea and a snug kitten or two on your lap next to the woodstove — is all you need to take you back to a simpler place in time — a place that is not forgotten.

Blessed be, my sweet friends.
– Lori

Always remember that handwork is something to be enjoyed — not rushed, and it shouldn't have to be perfect.

Notforgotten Farm › Introduction

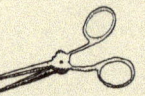

INSTRUCTIONS

Basic Instructions

The projects in this book were designed assuming the reader has basic knowledge of rug hooking, wool appliqué, counted cross stitch, hand sewing and punch needle. Here are a few things I do that may help you achieve that wonderful, old look to your finished project.

AGING COTTON FABRIC

I hand wash the fabric in hot water using mild dish soap and a cool rinse. Once it has been rinsed well, I hang it out on the line in full sun to help fade it a bit. I sometimes wash a bunch of fat quarters like this at one time and hang them all out on the line for a couple of days, letting the sun fade them nicely – and they look so pretty hanging on my line!

Once the fabric has been dried and faded, I then use a fine grit sandpaper on the fabric, rubbing gently in spots being careful not to rip the threads of the fabric. This adds a little more age to it.

After sanding, I then stain the fabric using a weak bath of coffee, tea or walnut stain. This will lend an aged look to it and help 'mellow' the colors.

To stain the fabric, I place an old towel on my work surface. Placing the fabric, facing up, on top of the towel, I then use an old bristle paintbrush and dip it into the dye bath. Next, I brush the dye onto the fabric on random places where I want staining to occur.

I don't like to dip my fabric directly into the dye, because I want the look to replicate an actual stain. Dry the fabric in the sun or on a cookie sheet in a low oven. The heat from the sun and/ or oven will cause the tannins in the dye to darken. Reapply more stain as desired for the effect you'd like to obtain.

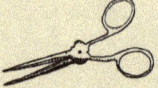

HAND STITCHING

I prefer to hand stitch my work, but will occasionally use my sewing machine for larger work.

I use plain cotton thread in brown, natural or linen color. I use simple embroidery needles because of their larger eyes (easier for my eyes to thread!) and I don't worry about what size my stitches are or if they're perfect or not – that is the beauty of something made by hand.

Instead of working with heavier perle cottons or floss, I prefer to use cotton thread for all of my appliqué. I simply stitch around the appliqué with a primitive whip stitch. I like the finished look of this, and it lends itself nicely to my simple designs.

RUG HOOKING

I pull wool loops through a linen backing. Simple as that. There is no magic involved in rug hooking – no secret technique. My loops are not even and my wool strips are not all the same size width, because I choose to hand cut them using Fiskars spring-loaded scissors. I try to use recycled wools, but I love the wools on the market that are milled specifically for rug hooking.

I love how an old hooked rug looks – made by someone long ago from spent clothing. Made to warm the floors of their home, the motifs were drawn simply and naively, and that, to me, is true folk art.

PUNCH NEEDLE

Punch needle is a somewhat newer needlecraft to our list, although it has been around for centuries. Believed to have been first used by Native Americans wanting to adorn their ceremonial garb, these creative people used hollow bird-bones fashioned into needles. We now know it to be a very rewarding, inexpensive form of needlework that is very portable. Punch needle takes a bit more practice, but once you get the hang of it, you will love it.

Cross Stitch

CROSS STITCH

Now here is where my technique may differ from others. When I learned to cross stitch, I was advised to find the center of my design and fabric, and start stitching in the center. Nope, not for me! I find it much easier to begin stitching in either an upper left or lower left corner of the design and work my way out from there. If there is a border, I start stitching it from either the upper or lower left, and then complete it. Then I move onto the motifs, letters, numbers, etc. It works for me, as I can gauge my fabric size better that way — and since I work my cross stitch on linen, it helps me waste less of it. Those of you who stitch on linen know that it can be expensive, especially hand-dyed linen.

My designs for cross stitch are stitched on linen, using one strand of floss over two threads of linen. I almost always use DMC floss for my work — it is inexpensive, found at almost every hobby/craft store and is color fast. I love to stain my finished cross stitch projects after they're completed, and by using DMC floss, it helps to know that the floss colors will not bleed or run.

When I use hand dyed threads, Gentle Art Sampler Threads and Weeks Dye Works threads are my choices.

Perhaps a steaming hot cup of pine needle tea and a snug kitten or two on your lap next to the woodstove is all you need to take you back to a simpler place in time — a place that is not forgotten.

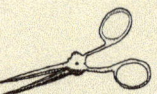

Supplies

SUPPLIES FOR THE PROJECTS IN THIS BOOK CAN BE FOUND AT THESE SHOPS:

Cottonwood Quilt Shop
2035 Barracks Road
Charlottesville, VA 22903
Phone: (434) 244-9975
Email: shop@cottonwoodquiltshop.com
Fabrics, notions

Quilted Expressions
3622 Old Forest Road
Lynchburg, VA 24501
Phone: (434) 385-6765
Fabrics, notions

Notforgotten Farm
3530 Tye River Road
Amherst, VA 24521
Email: not4got@aol.com
Web: www.farmhousenotforgotten.blogspot.com
Old Farmhouse Linen, Cameo Ultra punch needles, original patterns for cross stitch and punch needle, organic sawdust

PUNCH NEEDLE

Bittersweet

Ditty Bag
Designed and made by Lori Brechlin
Finished punch needle: 5" × 7"
Finished bag size: 8½" × 10½"

NEEDFULS

1 fat quarter weavers cloth in white

1 fat quarter cotton print in an autumnal color for the bag

Lip Lock Hoop or Gripper Frame

Cameo Ultrapunch needle, medium tip

Sewing needle

Cotton thread

Pins

Small, sharp scissors

DMC Floss

1 skein each:
400
780
976
831
732
610
612
3829
371
640
611

2 skeins each:
3021 background

4 to 5 skeins each:
310 outline

Notforgotten Farm › *Bittersweet Ditty Bag*

INSTRUCTIONS

This design uses 6 strands of DMC floss throughout the entire design and a Cameo Ultrapunch needle with a medium tip on the #2 setting.

Using the template found on page 15, trace the design onto weaver's cloth using a pencil, and place in the lip lock hoop or on the gripper frame, making sure weaver's cloth is drum-tight.

Punching the Design
Punch the design in the following order.

   976 for berries
   780 for berries
   400 for berries
   732 for leaves and "grass" below the bowl
   610 for the stripes on the bowl
   612 for the rest of the bowl
   3829 for scallops
   371 for scallops
   640 for remaining scallops

Background
Thread your needle with 310 and outline entire design twice, including the scallops and border.

Fill in the background with 310, leaving some open spots. Fill the empty spots with 3021.

Finishing
After punching is complete, remove your project from the hoop or frame. Trim away the excess weavers cloth to within ½" all the way around the last punched row of project. Turn the remaining weavers cloth to the back of the project and iron the remaining edge of the weavers cloth to the back of the punched project.

To make the Ditty Bag
Cut the fat quarter in half to make 2 pieces approximately 9" × 11". Pin them, right sides together. Using a ¼" seam allowance, sew along 3 sides, leaving the top, short end open. Turn the bag right sides out.

Pin the finished punched project to the bag, centering on the front. Hand stitch the punched project to the front of the ditty bag.

To make the drawstring, thread the sewing needle with 22" of 6 strands of 611 floss. Use a running stitch and sew approximately ½" below the top edge along the top of the entire opening of the bag. Pull the floss so the bag closes slightly.

Notforgotten Farm › *Bittersweet Ditty Bag*

Bittersweet ditty bag template

WOOL APPLIQUÉ

Squash Blossom

Table Runner
Designed and made
by Lori Brechlin
Finished size: 12" × 39"

NEEDFULS

11 — 4" × 12" pieces of assorted cotton prints (4 dark, 4 medium, 3 light) for the background

1 — 40" × 15" piece cotton print fabric for the backing

Assorted scrap wools in blue; light, medium and dark green; white; brown; and mustard

Cotton thread

Sewing needle

Pins

White copy paper

INSTRUCTIONS

Background
Machine or hand stitch the background prints together, using ¼" seam allowance, stitching together the long sides. Refer to the photo as your guide. Press the seams open and set aside.

Wool Appliqué
Trace all templates found on pages 18–19 onto the copy paper. Cut out and trace the templates onto the corresponding wools and cut out on the line.

Find the center of your stitched background by folding in half widthwise and finger press. Center and pin the blue wool heart to the crease of the runner.

Referring to the photo to the right and on page 11, pin your wool pieces to the background and stitch in place using cotton thread and a primitive whip stitch. Everything doesn't have to match perfectly, so please don't fret if one of your stems is a bit wonkier than the other, or if one leaf is lower than the next. You want this to look handmade.

Finishing
Once all of your wool pieces are stitched in place, press the front of your appliquéd runner with a hot iron. Now lay your backing fabric face down on your work surface, and your runner face up on top of that, centering the runner top on the backing fabric and pin in place.

Cut the backing fabric to within 1" all around the edges of the runner top, and fold over twice and stitch the border edge down using a primitive whip stitch and cotton thread.

You may age this project further by dabbing on a little coffee, tea or walnut stain and letting it dry in the sun.

Notforgotten Farm › *Squash Blossom Table Runner*

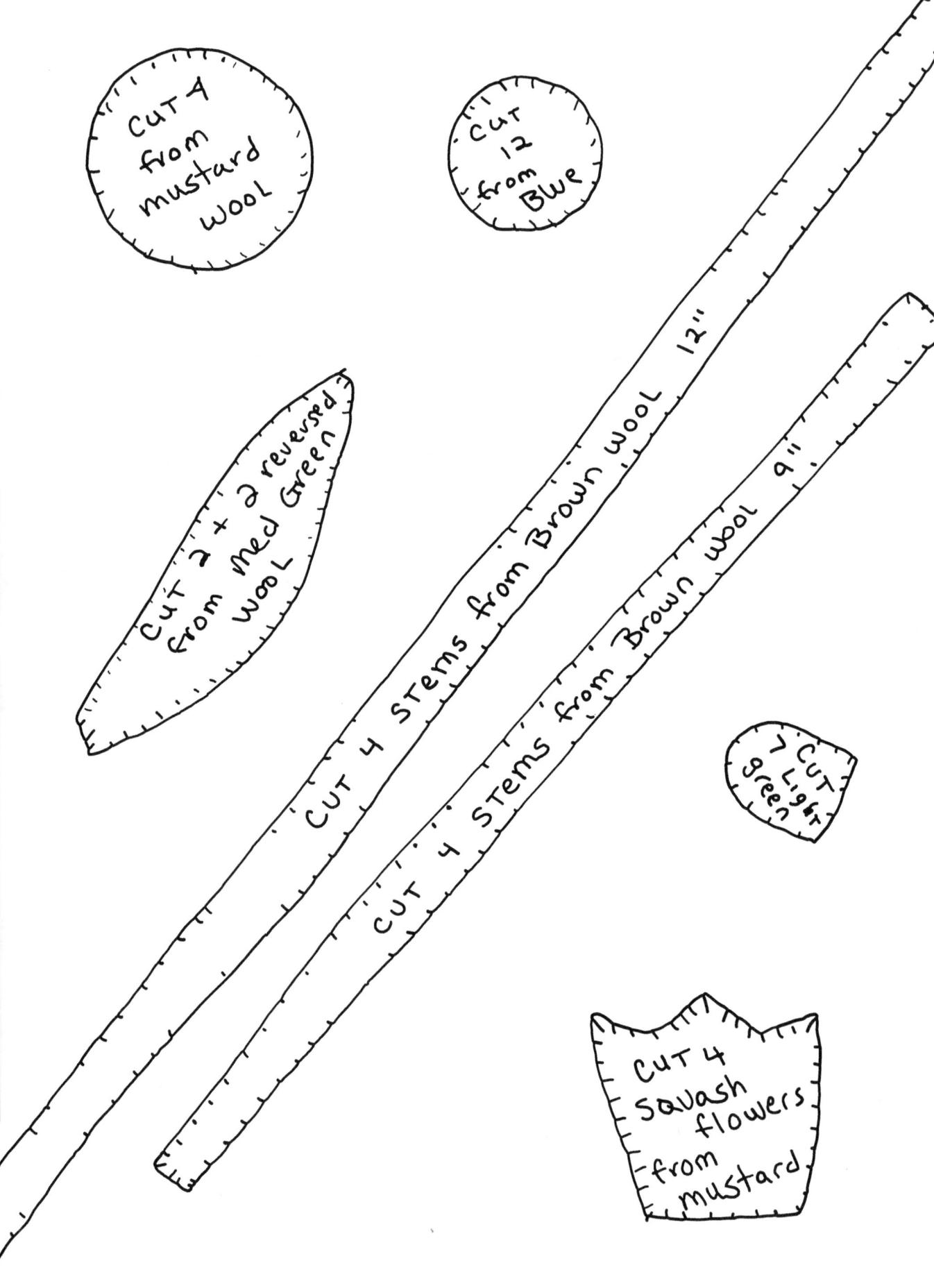

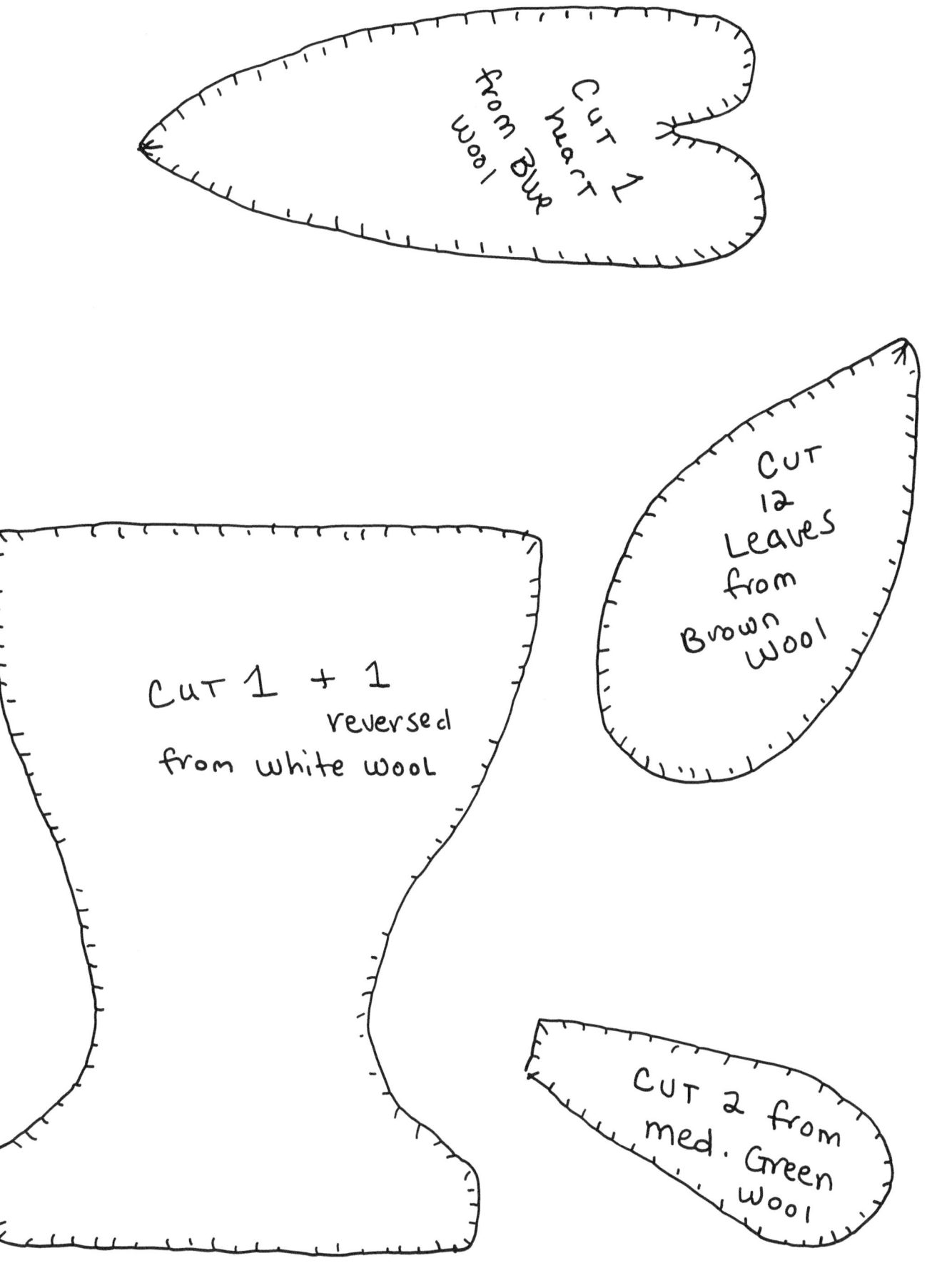

Squash Blossom Table Runner ‹ Notforgotten Farm

CROSS STITCH

Turkey Trot

Pillow
Finished size: 9" × 6"
Stitch count: 135W × 89H
Designed by Lori Brechlin
Made by Felicia Martin

NEEDFULS

11" × 8" of 30ct. Old Farmhouse Linen from Notforgotten Farm, see supplies on page 11.

11" × 8" piece of cotton print for pillow backing

Needle

Thread

Scissors

Organic sawdust for stuffing

SYMBOLS / DMC COTTON FLOSS

1 skein each

Symbol	DMC	Color
–	611	drab brown
⊂	782	dark topaz
⊃	831	medium golden olive
⁄⁄	3021	very dark brown-gray
π	3033	very light mocha brown
⁄	3828	hazelnut brown

Notforgotten Farm › *Turkey Trot Pillow*

INSTRUCTIONS

Cross stitch with 1 strand of cotton over 2 threads of linen.

Finishing

Press the finished cross stitch from the backside and lay it face down on your work surface. Using a pencil and ruler, draw a line 1" from the cross stitch on all 4 sides.

Lay the cotton backing fabric face up on your work surface, and lay your finished project face down, centered on top.

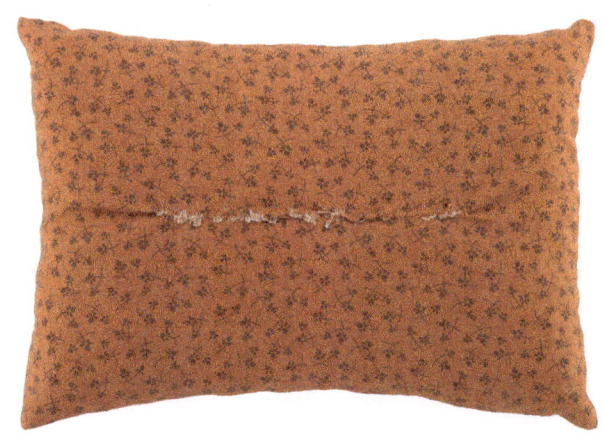

Pin together the project and cotton fabric and sew on the drawn line all the way around. After sewing, cut away the excess linen and fabric, leaving a ½" seam allowance around the stitched line.

Cut a 4" slit in the backing fabric, being careful not to cut the front project. Turn right sides out and stuff firmly with sawdust, being careful to stuff all 4 corners well. Hand stitch the opening closed using cotton thread.

Notforgotten Farm › *Turkey Trot Pillow*

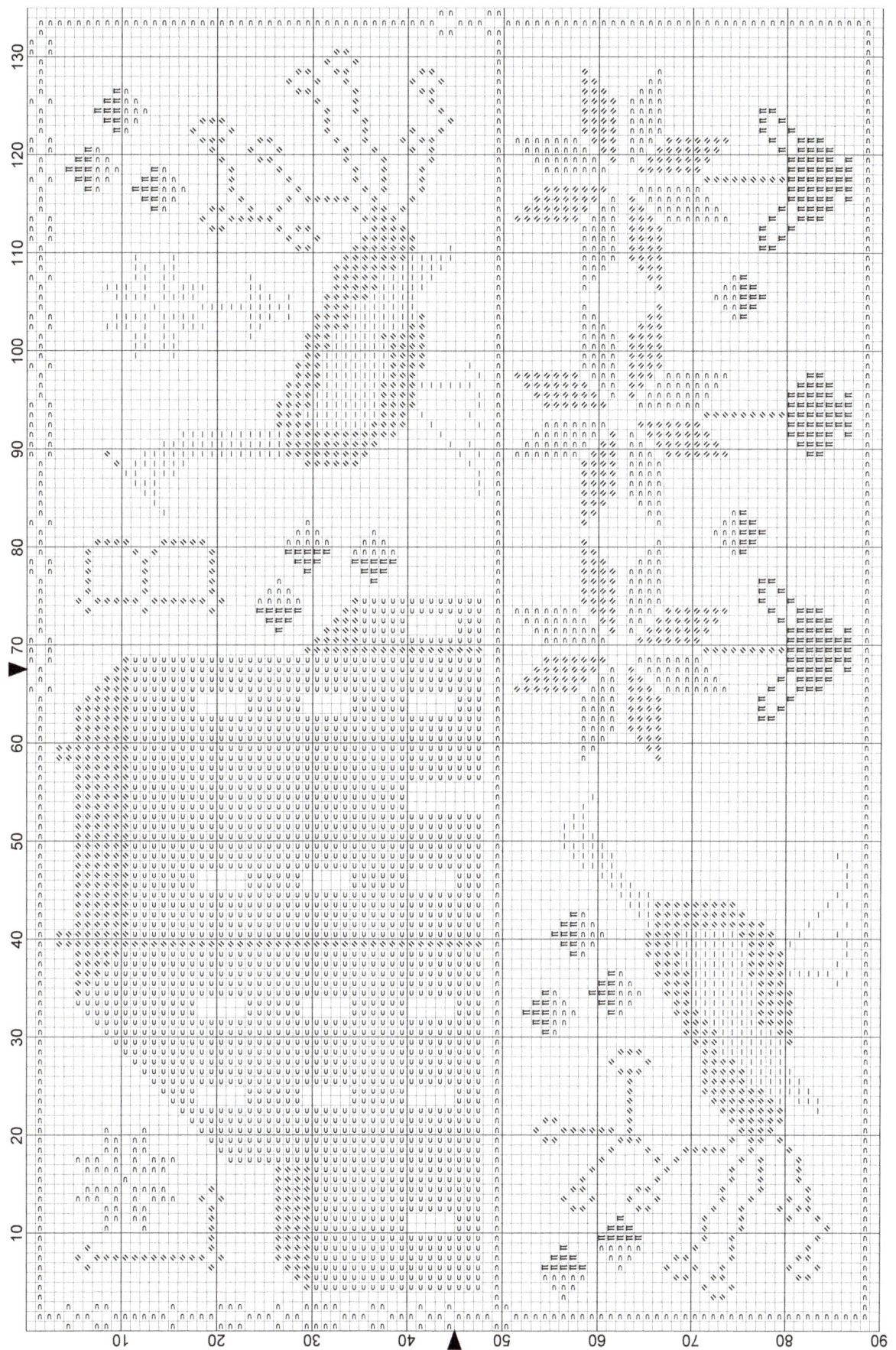

Turkey Trot Pillow ‹ Notforgotten Farm

HOOKED WOOL

Gathering Basket

Chair Pad
Designed and made by Lori Brechlin
Finished size: 12" diameter

NEEDFULS

- ½ yard of rug hooking foundation: linen, burlap or monk's cloth
- ⅛ yard of green wool for leaves
- ⅛ yard of orange wool for berries
- ¼ yard of greenish brown wool for stems
- ¼ yard of assorted brown wools for basket
- ½ yard total of assorted black wools for lettering and background
- Red dot tracer tracing paper or pellon pattern transfer fabric
- Black Sharpie marker
- Sharp scissors
- Rotary cutter and mat or wool cutter
- Large quilters hoop or Gripper rug frame
- Heavy black crochet thread

INSTRUCTIONS

Hooking

Using the template found on pages 27–29, trace the pattern onto the rug backing of your choice using tracing paper or transfer fabric and a black Sharpie. Make sure to leave at least 4" of foundation around the edge of the chair pad circle line.

Cut your wool into ¼" strips using a rotary cutter, scissors or wool cutter.

Begin hooking all the letters in the wording first, then move on to hook the smaller motifs such as berries, leaves, stems, etc. Next fill in basket. Now using black wools, hook completely around the drawn line of the chair pad circle and outline the entire design in black wool. Fill in the rest of the background using black wool.

Finishing

Once hooking is completed, dampen a small towel with water and lay it on the loops of the project. Using a hot iron, steam your project so the loops lay nicely. Let the project dry if it gets damp.

Trim away the excess foundation to within 1" completely around the last hooked row.

Fold the foundation once toward the back. You may need to make small slits in the foundation to help it lie flat, but don't slit into the last hooked row!

Turn back once more for a neat edge and whip-stitch the edge using the heavy black crochet thread.

You can age your chair pad by brewing a cup of strong tea or coffee and dabbing it onto the loops, letting the stain seep in a bit. Let it dry outside in the sun.

Be sure to stitch your name or initials into the back edge for future generations.

Notforgotten Farm › *Gathering Basket Chair Pad*

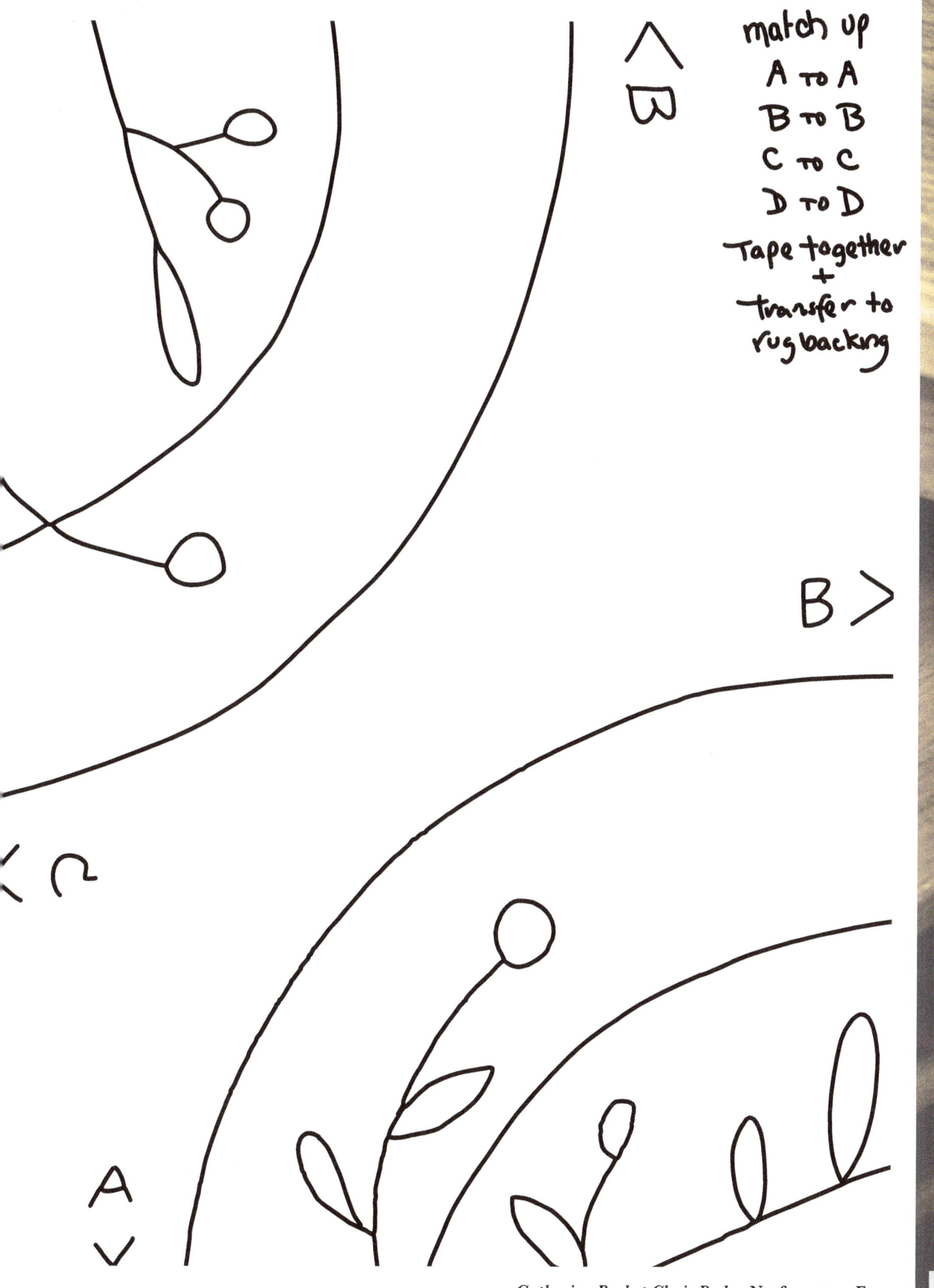

Notforgotten Farm › *Gathering Basket Chair Pad*

Gathering Basket Chair Pad ‹ Notforgotten Farm

WOOL APPLIQUÉ

Autumn

Banner
Designed and made by Lori Brechlin

NEEDFULS

6 — 6" × 8" pieces assorted cotton calico prints in varying shades of cream, off-white or tan

6 — 6" × 8" pieces of cotton calico prints in muted orange

6 — 5" × 7" pieces of wool: 3 browns, 1 gray, 1 black and 1 white for lettering

1 — 42" piece of heavy crochet string, ribbon or yarn

Sewing needle

Pins

Cotton thread

Small sharp scissors

Pencil

Chalk

White copy paper

INSTRUCTIONS

Wool Appliqué

Begin by tracing the lettering onto the white paper using a pencil. Cut out the paper letter templates on the line and pin to the corresponding wool color. Using the chalk, trace around each paper letter template onto the wool and cut out the wool letter. Set aside.

Place all 6 pieces of muted orange cotton prints face up on your worktable. Place all 6 pieces of assorted cotton prints face down on top of the muted orange fabric pieces.

Trace the banner "tongue" template onto the white paper and cut it out. Place the paper template onto each piece of doubled fabric on your worktable and trace the edge all the way around using a pencil. Hand or machine stitch each tongue where indicated on the pattern, leaving the top open.

Clip each tongue on the stitched curve and turn them right side out. Press each one with a hot iron.

Place the wool letters on top of the stitched tongue, centering and measuring the bottom of each letter to within approximately ¾" from the bottom of each tongue. Pin the wool letter in place on each tongue.

Using a needle and thread, stitch each letter to its tongue using a small, primitive whip stitch. Stitch completely through the double fabric tongue.

Notforgotten Farm › *Autumn Banner*

Finishing

Once all of your letters are stitched onto the tongues, place the 42" piece of ribbon, yarn or string on your worktable. Place your appliquéd tongues on top of the ribbon, spaced evenly approximately 2" apart and with the tops of the tongues measuring approximately 1" covering the ribbon from the top. You will fold over the tops of each tongue to the back, covering the ribbon and pinning it so it doesn't slide on the ribbon. Stitch each tongue into place along the ribbon either by hand or machine.

Once you've stitched all the tongues to the ribbon, make a loop and knot at each end to hang.

You can further age your finished banner by dabbing it with strong coffee or tea or your stain of preference and set in the sun to dry.

Hang your finished banner where you can welcome AUTUMN to your warm, cozy home! Mine hangs on our mantle in the keeping room of our farmhouse.

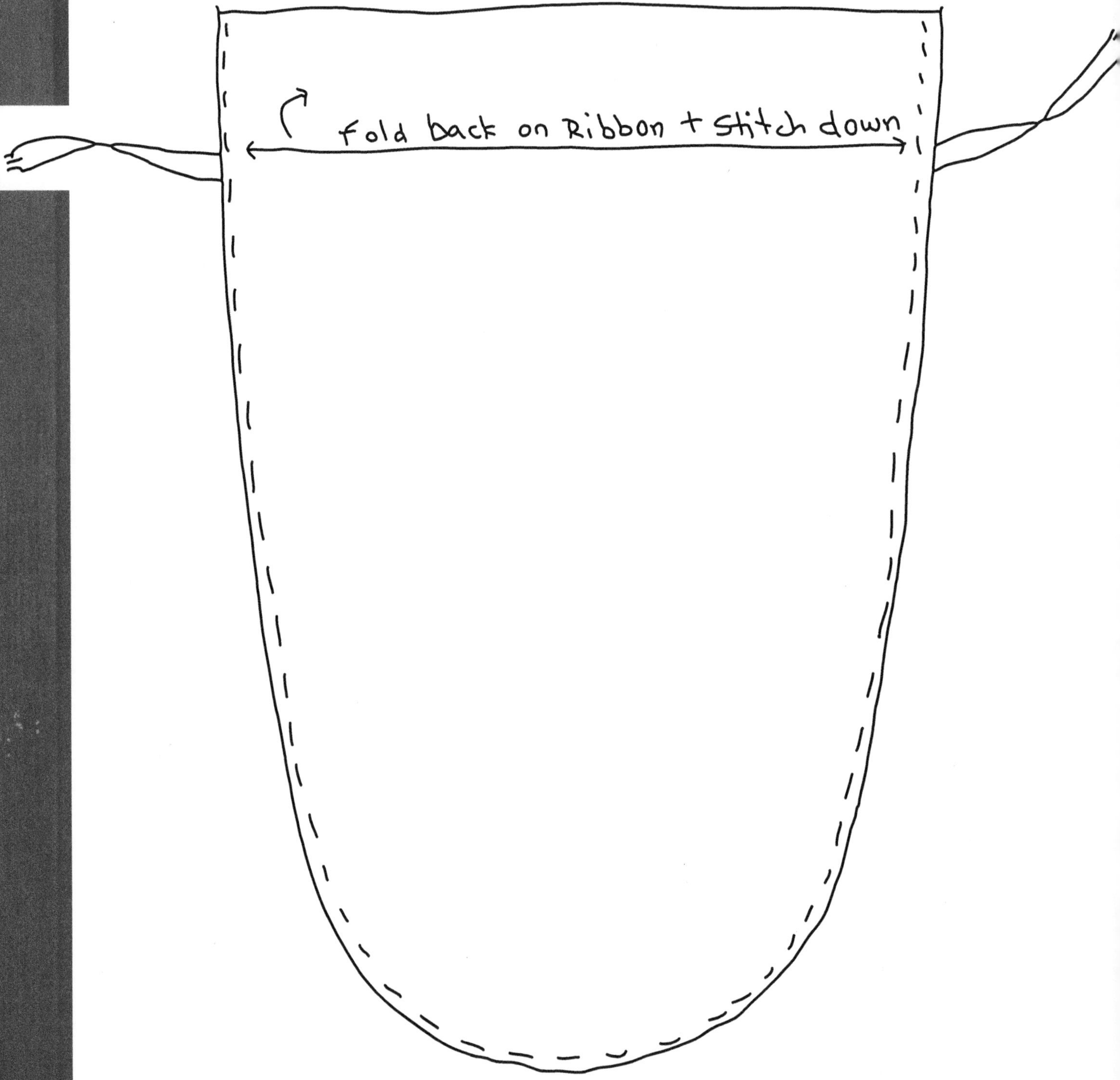

Fold back on Ribbon + Stitch down

Notforgotten Farm › *Autumn Banner*

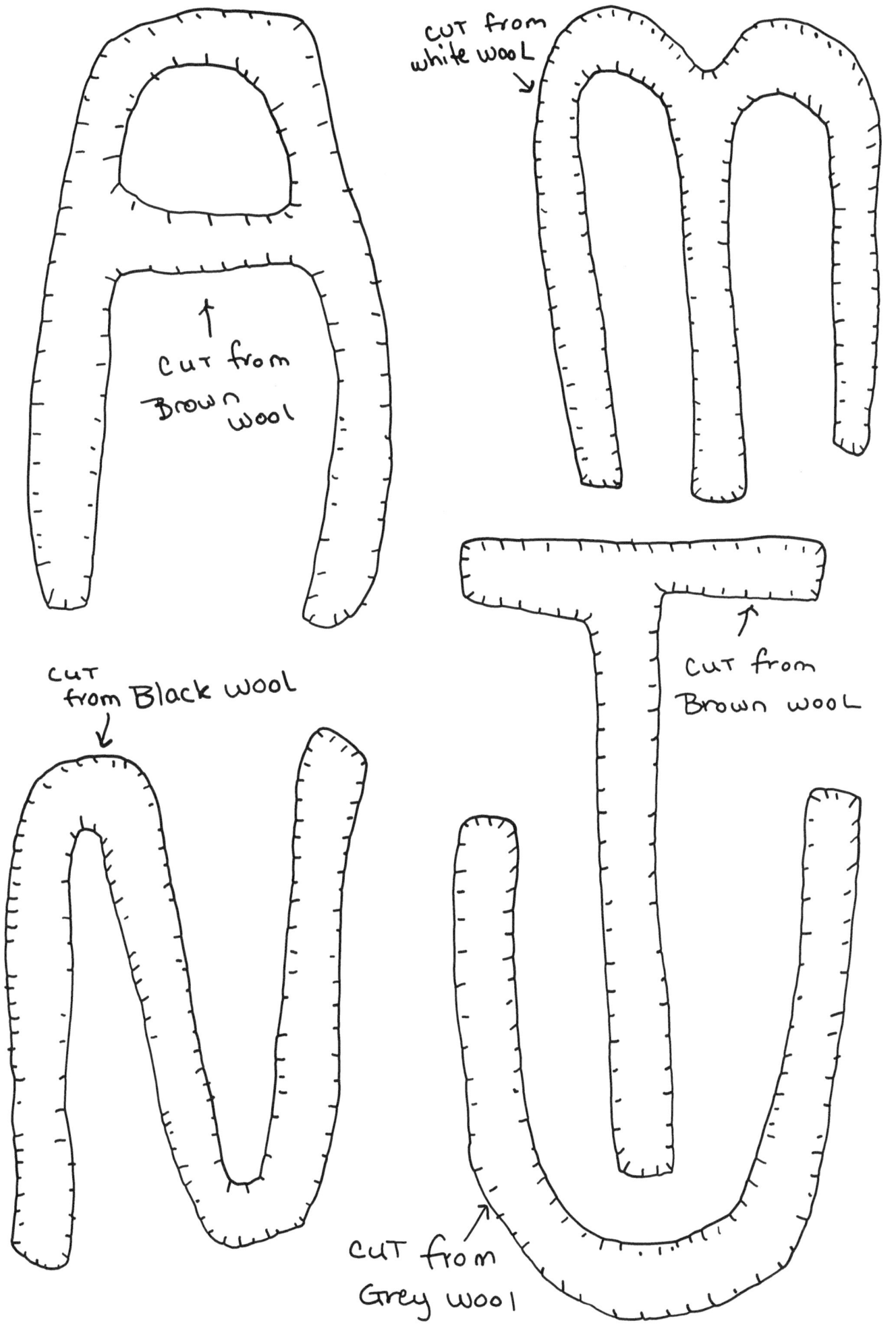

CROSS STITCH

September's Blessing

Framed Sampler

Finished design size: 7½" × 7½"

Stitch count: 112W × 112H

Designed by Lori Brechlin

Made by Felicia Martin

NEEDFULS

12" × 12" piece of 30ct Old Farmhouse Linen from Notforgotten Farm, see supplies on page 11.

14" square of orange wool

15" square wooden frame

Black acrylic paint

Colonial blue acrylic paint

Elmer's brand spray adhesive

Medium grit sandpaper

Brown Minwax

Needle

Thread

Scissors

Sawdust for stuffing

SYMBOLS / DMC COTTON FLOSS

1 skein each

Symbol	DMC	Color
u	422	light hazel nut brown
⊃	831	medium golden olive
△	946	medium burnt orange
⁄⁄	3021	very dark brown gray
+	3031	very dark mocha brown
∿	3828	hazel nut brown
2	3852	very dark straw
1	Ecru	ecru
4	732	olive green
8	400	dark mahogany
•	924	very dark gray green

Notforgotten Farm › *September's Blessing Framed Sampler*

INSTRUCTIONS

Cross stitch with 1 strand of cotton over 2 threads of linen.

Finishing

Using a pencil and ruler, draw a line 1" from the cross stitch on all 4 sides and cut it out on the line. Hem the sides of the sampler with a running stitch and cotton thread to match the background.

Cut the cardboard to the opening dimension of the frame. Spray a light coat of spray adhesive to it. Once tacky, lay the wool on top and cut around the edges to fit the cardboard leaving about 1" on all 4 sides.

Center the sampler on the wool-covered cardboard. Stitch the sampler to the wool using a large, thin needle and cotton thread. Place in the frame to finish.

Preparing the frame

You can use a finished frame or an antique frame for this project. I found an unfinished frame at our local craft store and painted it.

To finish the frame as I did, first paint the frame with a basecoat of black acrylic paint. Once dried, paint it with a colonial blue acrylic paint. Run a comb through the wet paint to show the basecoat underneath. Once dry, sand the frame on the corners and edges and seal it with Minwax.

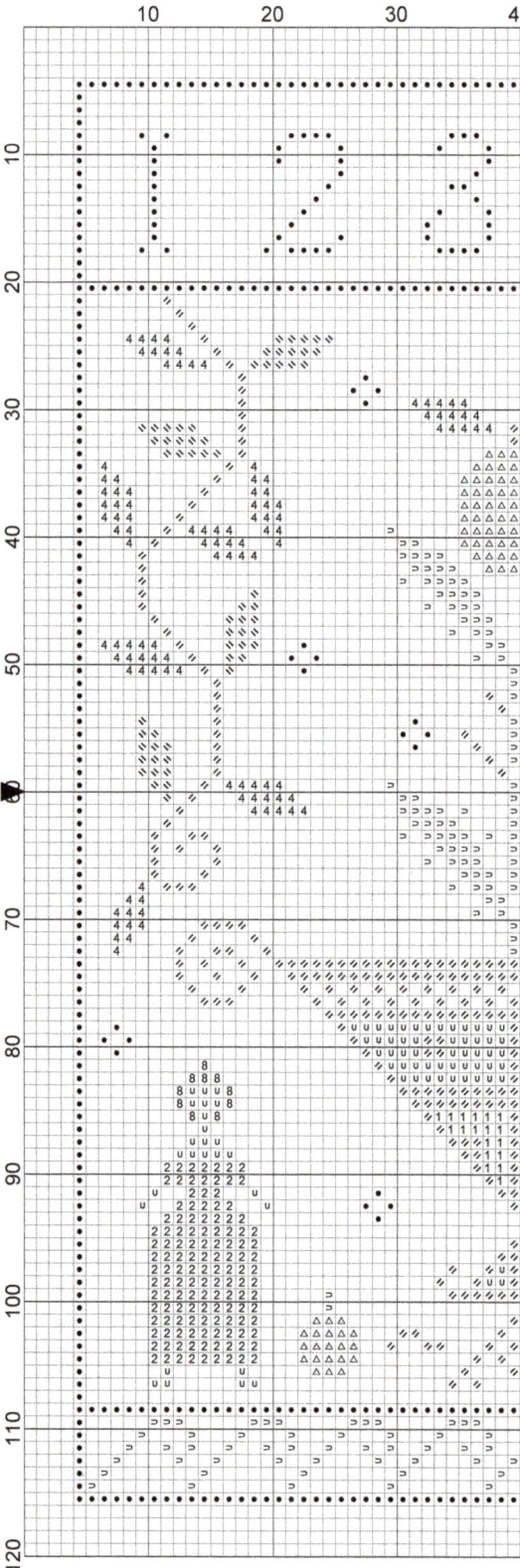

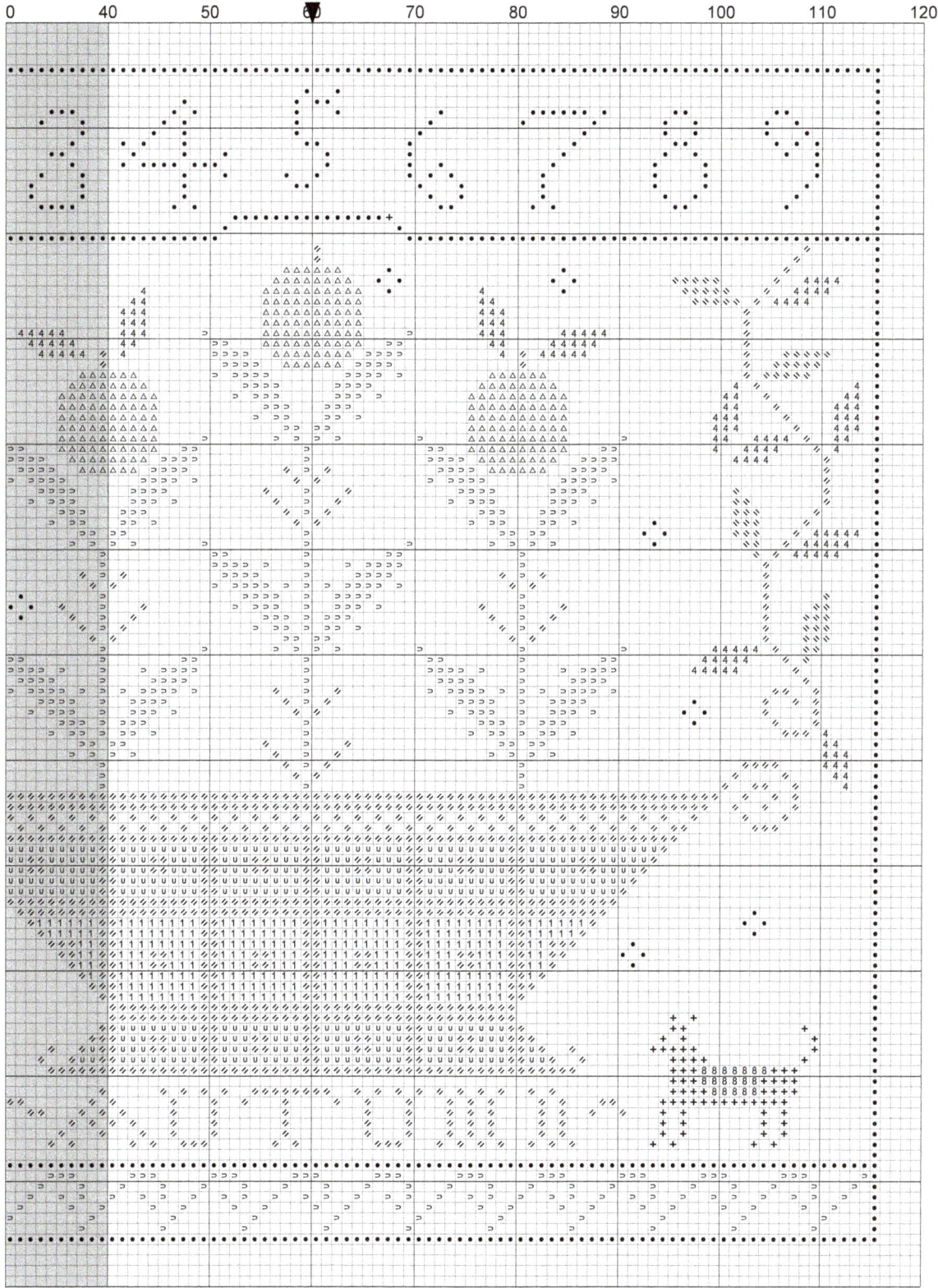

gray indicates repeat

September's Blessing Framed Sampler ‹ Notforgotten Farm

SIMPLE SEWING PROJECT

Calico Shoe Thimble Keep

Necklace
Designed and made by Lori Brechlin

NEEDFULS

2 — 6" × 6" pieces of cotton prints in your choice of color

Cotton or Polyfil for stuffing

Small white knitters ring

26" long piece of hemp cord or heavy crochet thread for necklace

Sewing needle

Cotton thread

Sharp scissors

Sewing pins

1 large and 1 small bone or mother of pearl button

INSTRUCTIONS

Place the 2 pieces of calico fabric on your work surface right sides together. Using the template found on page 43, trace the shoe template onto white paper and cut out leaving a ¼" seam allowance around the template. Trace the shoe template onto the wrong side of the top cotton fabric using a pencil. Pin the fabric pieces together.

Referring to the pattern template, hand stitch around the shoe template on fabric using a needle and thread, leaving the top of the "tube" open. Turn the shoe right side out.

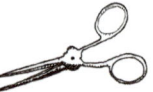

Stuff the toe of the shoe firmly with cotton or Polyfil, then proceed to stuff the heel. After stuffing the heel a bit, add more stuffing where needed. Then stitch the top of the "tube" closed and poke it down into the shoe itself. Use your finger to create more of a space for the thimble.

Using your needle and thread, make tiny stitches completely around the opening of where you will place the thimble.

Stitch the white knitters ring to the back of the shoe just above the heel, using cotton thread.

Thread the string through the ring and tie the ends of the string or cord through the large button. Stitch a small button to the top front of the shoe.

Stick in a few large pins and slip in your thimble. Wear proudly!

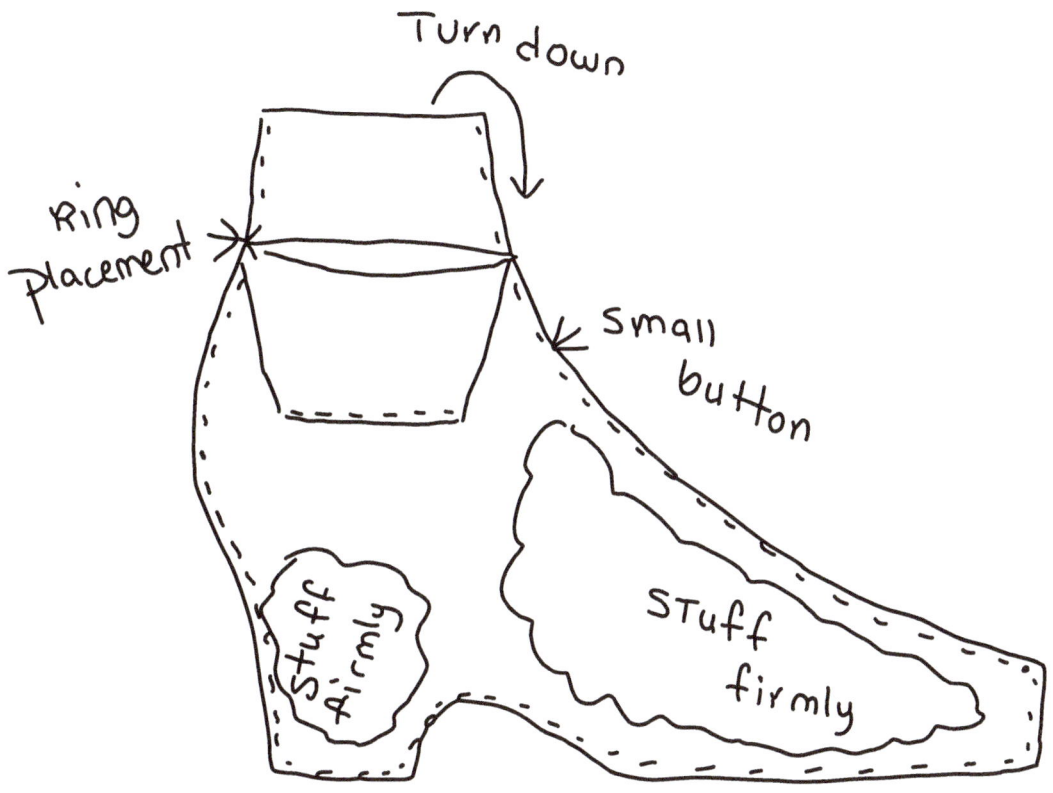

Calico Shoe Thimble Keep template

CROSS STITCH

Old Farmhouse

Sampler

Finished design size: 7¾" × 7"

Finished size: 9¾" × 9"

Stitch count: 116W × 105H

Designed by Lori Brechlin

Made by Felicia Martin

NEEDFULS

11" square of 30ct Old Farmhouse Linen from Notforgotten Farm, see supplies on page 11.

11" square of cotton print for backing

Needle

Thread

Scissors

Organic sawdust for stuffing

SYMBOLS | DMC COTTON FLOSS

1 skein each

Symbol	DMC	Color
−	611	drab brown
ɔ	831	medium golden olive
″	3021	very dark brown gray
1	Ecru	ecru
8	400	dark mahogany

INSTRUCTIONS

Cross stitch with 1 strand of cotton over 2 threads of linen.

Finishing

Press the finished cross stitch from the backside and lay it face down on your work surface. Using a pencil and ruler, draw a line 1" from the cross stitch on all 4 sides.

Notforgotten Farm › *Old Farmhouse Sampler*

Lay the cotton backing fabric face up on your work surface, and lay your finished project face down, centered on top.

Pin together the project and cotton fabric and sew on the drawn line all the way around. After sewing, cut away the excess linen and fabric, leaving a ½" seam allowance around the stitched line.

Cut a 2" slit in the backing fabric, being careful not to cut the front project. Turn right sides out and stuff firmly with sawdust, being careful to stuff all 4 corners well. Hand stitch the opening closed using cotton thread.

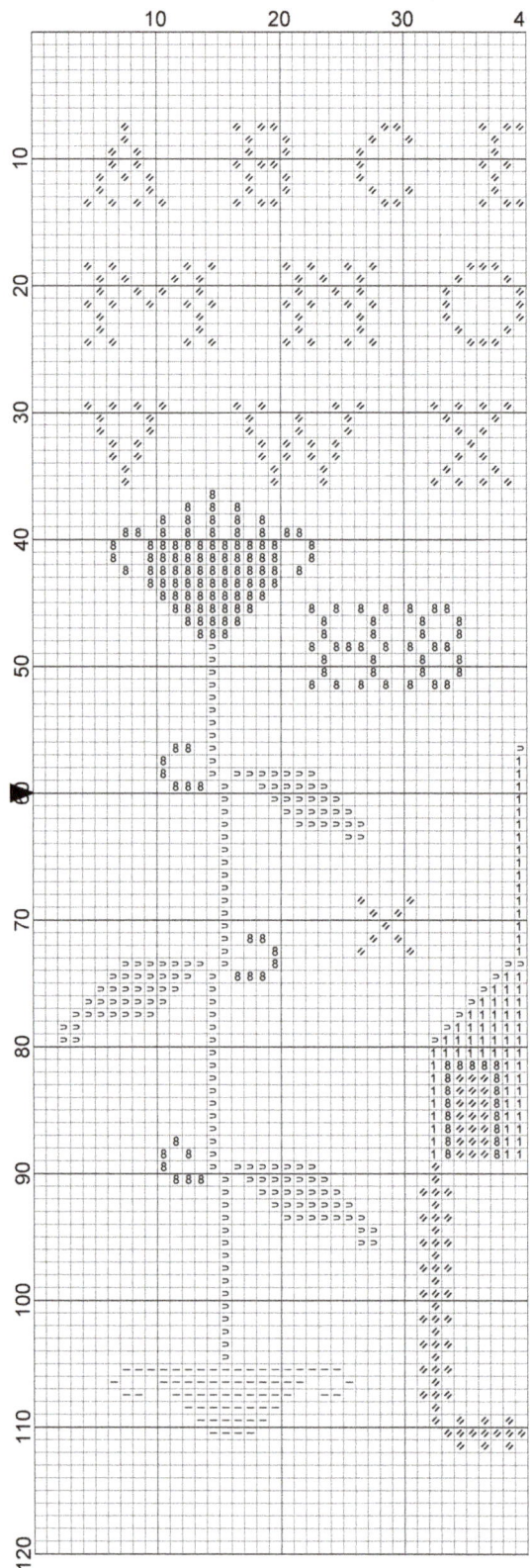

Notforgotten Farm › *Old Farmhouse Sampler*

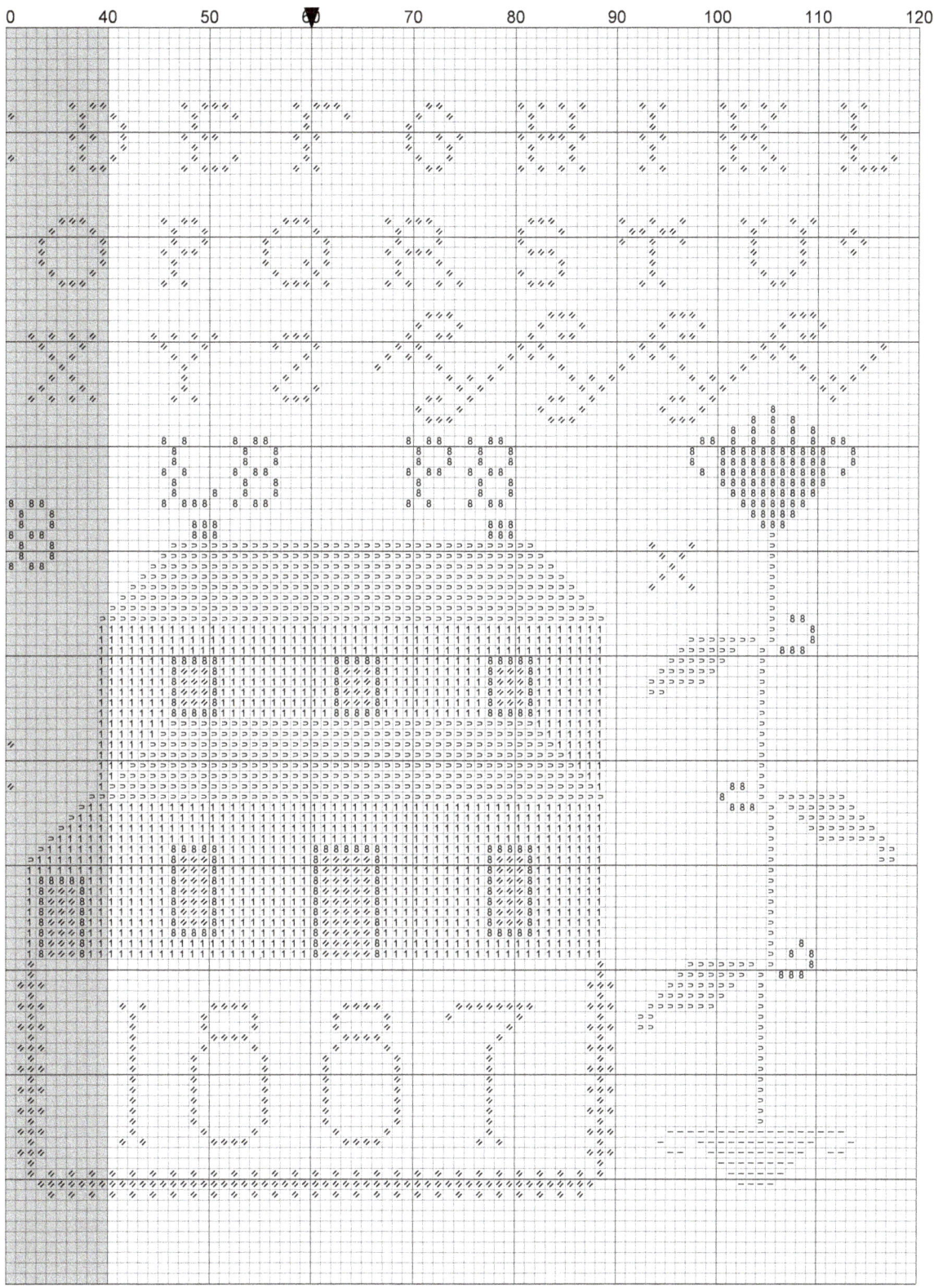

gray indicates repeat

Old Farmhouse Sampler ‹ Notforgotten Farm

About the Author

Lori Brechlin

I grew up in Connecticut, loving the smell of the woods and the smell of salt air — I loved to take long walks in the ancient cemeteries and study crumbling headstones, their hand carved artwork stirring something in my old soul.

I can remember visiting homes of friends and relatives and seeing old samplers, hooked rugs and sewing items lovingly displayed. I loved to visit my aunts' homes, which were decorated much like I decorate today — with things made by hand, from their heart — made with not much money, but with much love.

My mom's side of the family is Pennsylvania German, and I think I gain most of my inspiration for my work from there. My favorite colors are soot, bone white, moss and sage greens, oxblood red, dirty brown, yellow ochre and robin's egg blue.

I love to sit in our old farmhouse when it is raining and stitch something, listening to the melody of raindrops on our tin roof.

I have a fondness for old and worn things — leather children's shoes and clothing, fraying and tattered samplers under old wavy glass and rugs hooked from spent clothing, made to warm the floors of early farmhouse kitchens.

I collect scraps of fabrics, balls of twine and yellowing ironstone. I gravitate towards dusty books and ripped upholstery, seeing not their imperfections, but their unique ability to calm and relax me.

I am forever finding inspiration from antique needlework and from Mother Nature — and I love all animals.

I hope the designs in this book inspire you to make something that will fill your heart. I am always available by email at not4got@aol.com if you ever have any questions.

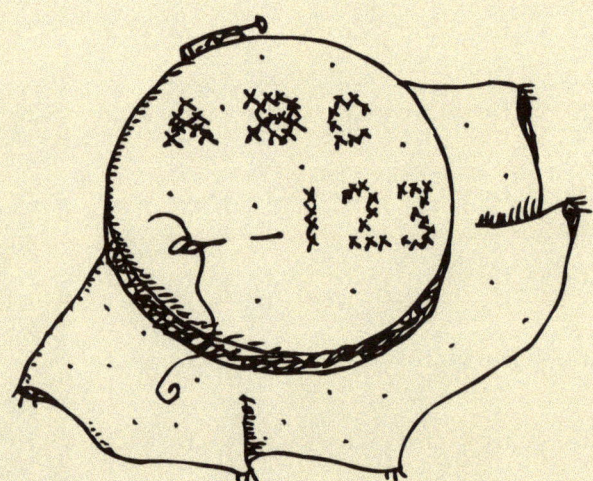

www.ingramcontent.com/pod-product-compliance
Lightning Source LLC
Chambersburg PA
CBHW060950170426
43202CB00026B/3002